HISTORIC ISLE OF WIGHT FOOD

JAMES RAYNER

James

To Melik, Mum and Mr Smith

First published in 2021.

ISBN 9781527293397

Typeset and printed by All Things Printed Ltd,
The Innovation Centre, St. Cross Business Park, Newport, Isle of Wight, PO30 5WB.

Contents

Introduction

Today, the Isle of Wight is renowned for its food. Our 150 square miles of land are home to dozens of skilled artisans, talented small producers, dedicated fishermen and passionate farmers. Locally grown products have become nationally recognised and prominent chefs and food writers frequently visit our shores. However, it's quite a modern phenomenon.

What is missing from the Island's current culinary offering is a more historic food culture, one based on tradition and history. Unlike Yorkshire, Cumbria, Wales or Scotland, the Isle of Wight doesn't make regional specialities based on recipes first written or created hundreds of years ago. There are no famous pies or pastries named after our towns or villages and no ancient cheeses that have been awarded with protected status.

But this doesn't mean that the Island has no historic food culture - it does, it's just waiting to be revived.

In fact, the Isle of Wight has all the elements it needs to establish (or re-establish) it's own regional cuisine. The components that make up Basque, Sicilian or Punjabi cuisine, such as a different landscape to the rest of the nation, a different food heritage, culture and dialect, can also be seen as true for the Island as well.

The only challenge is that the Isle of Wight's links to its culinary history have been severed for over one hundred years. At the time, there was no proper record of the Island's food customs and today there is no-one left to ask how things were done. All we have to work from are the dialect dictionaries, botanical reference books, biographies, tour guides and newspaper articles from the 19th century and earlier, which give us brief glimpses into the Island's forgotten past.

A lot of what took place will remain a mystery and some things will no doubt be lost forever, however, by using what we have available to us, we can start to reconstruct a picture of what Islanders ate and drank over the past centuries. We can find out how dialect words were used to describe cooking techniques, we can discover what herbs were growing wild on the Downs and what special cakes Islanders baked for Shrove Tuesday and All Hallows' Eve.

This book uses hundreds of sources to start patching this picture together but in truth, it's only scratching the surface. Nevertheless, it creates a foundation onto which a revived culinary culture based on tradition and history can be established.

Reconstructing the Island's Historic Food Culture

The historic characteristics of Isle of Wight food certainly contained a unique mix of different elements, some shared with others regions, some specific to the Island. Together they combined to create a distinctive regional cuisine, which in some respects, was partly recognised at the time.

To begin with, the Island's varied landscape is certainly different from much of the rest of the UK and the edible plants native to the Island are even noticeably different from those found on the other side of the Solent.

For example, over a hundred years ago both juniper and wild chamomile were commonly found growing in Hampshire but pretty much non-existent on the Island. On the other hand, wild bullaces, horehound, sour cherries, black mustard, gillyflowers and sea cabbage were all abundant on the Isle of Wight but rare or completely missing from the wild plants of Hampshire.

Even within the Island's landscape there was variation, mackerel was only caught off the Back of the Wight, chequers only found on the north side of the Island and bilberries only grew on a select few heaths and downlands. The wild plants available to Islanders create such a mismatched patchwork that it's even quite likely that Islanders in Freshwater and Bembridge may have cooked with a completely different variety of herbs, fruits and vegetables.

Secondly, the food heritage of the Isle of Wight is also different from the rest of the country. The Island had its own breed of pig, its very own variety of apple and a few original culinary creations too, such as the Isle of Wight Doughnut and the Isle of Wight Cracknel - which was known right across the UK during the 19th century. It also developed a reputation nationally for the quality of its butter, lamb, shrimps and cockles.

Compared to the people of Hampshire, Islanders used the ingredients around them in different ways and for different purposes too. In 1810, an agricultural report noted that very few Hampshire families used their apples to make cider and that it appeared 'nowhere to be an object of much concern amongst the rural inhabitants'. On the Island however, there were few farmers who didn't make from two to six hogsheads of excellent cider every year, saving a lot for themselves but also selling much of it to the Hampshire people who valued it highly and were willing to pay high prices to get hold of it. On the other hand, rearing beef cattle and growing rye were much rarer on the Island than across the water.

Furthermore, cultural differences also mark out the Isle of Wight's food history as distinct from other regions. Many of these differences are ancient in origin and very difficult to trace but we can find a mixture of ancient Celtic and later French influences that seem to have made an impression on the Island's cooking practices.

For one, there are definitely a number of similarities with Britain's Celtic cultures, especially Cornish and

Welsh, which may have been passed down from some of the Island's earliest inhabitants. The Isle of Wight's *vlitter* pancakes are similar to the Welsh buttermilk *crempog* pancakes and a number of local words, such as *plumper* (the name for a butter churn), as well as *bee butt* (for bee hive) and *stubberds* (a variety of apple) were also shared with the Cornish language or West Country dialects.

French influence is also noticeable but whether elements come from the Norman period or contact with mainland France is difficult to tell. Examples could include the local food names *merries*, *cracknels* and *junket* (said to come from the French words *merise*, *craquelin* and *jonquette*). In later years, contact with France became more frequent. The Island's own variety of apple, the Isle of Wight Pippin, was supposedly first brought across from Normandy, young oysters from Brittany were introduced into the Medina and during the early 19th century, much of the Island's spirits were smuggled over from the French coast via secret sailing expeditions.

It's also possible that the fact the Island was settled by Jutes (one of only two regions of Britain that were) as opposed to Angles or Saxons - may have left a mark too.

Over the following chapters, we'll take a tour of the lost world of Isle of Wight food. We'll bring to life the forgotten elements which characterised the regional cuisine of the Island in centuries past, from foraged fruit wine to *sand sprats* and samphire.

We'll also take a brief look at how the Island's ethnic minorities may have cooked and then see how later European trends would alter the Island's food scene forever.

A number of local recipes have been recreated, some using two hundred year old documents, while others that weren't recorded use the information available to best reconstruct what they might have looked like. Dialect food terms have been collected, as has a list of native or naturalised edible plants known to be growing on the Island in the 19th century.

Whilst there's still much more to be uncovered, this book starts to record some of the key features and characteristics that made Island food distinctive, providing an outline for the future, allowing this forgotten culinary history to be revived once again.

'He referred to the Isle
of Wight pippin, or
old orange apple, the
beautiful flavour of which
was lost when grown out
of the Island'

Fruit

Due to its abundance, variety and wide range of uses, fruit was possibly one of the most characteristic features of Isle of Wight food. Islanders foraged for rare and unusual fruits, used others to flavour alcohol and baked them into some of the Island's best known puddings and pastries. Some species flourished on the Island when they wouldn't elsewhere and even a few varieties native to the Middle East and Asia survived in the Undercliff's warm microclimate. However, of all the fruits that the Island produced, perhaps none were more useful and popular than the apple.

Two hundred years ago, apple trees could be found growing wild across most of the Island and where the soil was clay, apple orchards flourished too. Local people had a number of varieties to choose from when making their ciders and desserts, mainly crab apples, including *stubberds* (an early, green apple), *crumplen* (a small type with a wrinkled rind) and *rather ripe* (a variety that produced fruit earlier than all the others).

Aside from these, there was also the highly prized 'Isle of Wight Pippin', a cultivated variety of mysterious origin, which first appeared on the Island at some point in the

1700s. It was described as a 'first-rate dessert apple' and was also known as the 'Isle of Wight Orange' because of its colour - the ripe fruit said to look like a Seville orange.

Tradition states that the tree was introduced from Normandy and first planted at a house named 'Wraxhall Cottage' which was located near to the Undercliff. When exactly this happened is difficult to establish, but in 1831 there were trees growing on the Island that were already thought to be one hundred years old.

Sources described the apple as having a beautiful flavour which was lost when the tree was grown off the Island, and while there were other kinds of British apple known as 'Orange' or 'Orange Pippin', none could compete with the quality of the Isle of Wight variety.

Wild plums and damsons also grew abundantly throughout the Island - as did bullaces, which were found much more commonly on the Island than in Hampshire. The Ryde-based botanist, William Arnold Bromfield wrote in 1848 that he once brought home a quart of wild bullaces and had them made into a tart 'which was one of the best flavoured and most juicy I ever partook of'.

These fruits were mainly gathered and sold to make desserts, plums (locally called *kix* or *kecksies*) being used for cakes, puddings and Isle of Wight doughnuts, whilst damsons were used to make damson cheese - a preserve made from sugar and damsons, cooked together until they become the consistency of a soft cheese.

Sloes were a local favourite, often being used by Islanders to flavour spirits. In the 1890s, Frank Winter, a wine merchant from Ventnor, gained a reputation for his 'celebrated Isle of Wight Sloe Gin', a product he trademarked and which was prepared only from sloes grown on the Island. They were an incredibly abundant fruit as blackthorn hedges were often planted by farmers to mark their field boundaries, especially around Ryde, Nettlestone and Newchurch. Despite coming from the plum family, sloes were harvested much later in the year, so to distinguish them from wild plums, Islanders referred to them as *winter kecksies*.

Wild cherries (*prunus avium*) were commonly used to flavour alcohol too and could be found in many places across the Island. Locals knew them by the name of *merries* which was said to come from the French word *merise* and cherry orchards were known as *merry gardens*. In many places, the wild fruits were small, bitter and inedible but in the sandy soil at Borthwood, trees produced fruit that was described as 'black, sweet and excellently flavoured' which Island people sold at the market. The tangy flavoured sour cherry (*prunus cerasus*), could also be found on the Island in places such as Godshill, Brighstone and Chale, despite being a very rare tree over the water in Hampshire.

Strawberries, raspberries, blackberries and elderberries were abundant too, as were red currants, haws and rosehips. Pears grew here and there, and gooseberries (known as *goosegogs*) could be found wild in the woods.

Amongst the more unusual fruits which grew on the Island were chequers, the sharp-tasting fruit of the wild service tree (*sorbus torminalis*). They were mainly found on the north side of the Island, especially around Firestone, Quarr and Brock's Copse near Whippingham. The brown, dotted fruit, which locals called *sorbus berries*, ripened in October and November, and were sold at Ryde, tied up in small bunches.

On some heaths and downlands in south eastern parts of the Island, you could also find bilberries - the smaller, European cousin of the North American blueberry. A 19th century travel writer mentions that these fruits were 'known by a different name in the Isle of Wight' but it seems their exact name has not been recorded. In Hampshire, Dorset and Sussex, bilberries were known as *whorts*, *hart-berries* or *hurts* and gathering them was known as *hurting* or *whorting*, so it's possible the Island name was something along the same lines as well.

Some non-native fruits, originating in Asia or the Mediterranean, also thrived on the Island. Figs grew well in the Undercliff and in the 18th century a number of these trees were trained to form a canopy outside the New Inn at Steephill so visitors could dine on seafood *al fresco*. Quinces were not uncommon to find in cottage gardens and mulberries were harvested to make sweets such as the 'mulberry tart and a good jug of cream' mentioned by local author Maxwell Gray in her novel *Unconfessed*.

"Landcress... is generally thought to have been introduced to Europe from the New World... be that as it may, no plant is more thoroughly naturalised among us than the present, and in no part of Britain perhaps does it abound more than in this island..."

Vegetables, Herbs & Wild Plants

Most of the leaf and root vegetables grown on the Isle of Wight over a hundred and fifty years ago are still common these days, but others had more special importance or were prepared in different ways.

One of the staples of Island cooking were the young leaves and sprouts of cabbage - however, these weren't cabbages as we'd recognise them today and looked closer in form to modern kale or spring greens. Islanders knew them as *callards*, a word with the same origin as the American term *collard greens* (both of which stem from the Middle English name *colewort*).

On the Isle of Wight they were highly prized and formed a key part of many meals, often being served with ham or bacon. Different types of cabbage were also grown to supply the Island's hospitals as well as the markets of Portsmouth and Gosport, and much of the shipping in the Solent.

Another favourite were turnips (locally called *turmets*) which first appeared on the Island around the 1780s and quickly became one of the most popular vegetables at the time. They were useful not only for their white and purple roots but the *turnip greens* which grew on top.

More commonly known as turnip tops, the leaves have a

peppery, slightly lemony flavour and were frequently boiled
to provide the vegetable element of a meat-based meal. In
fact, judging by a number of newspaper articles, turnips and
turnip tops were one of the most commonly stolen crops
from Isle of Wight farms in the late 19th century. Thefts
like these no doubt prompted one West Wight landowner
to paint the following notice, as reported by William Henry
Long:

'Take notice
All you people that passes by,
Take a turmet if you be dry,
And if one won't do,
You may take two;
But if you takes three,
I'll take thee,
And into prison thee shalt be'.

Islanders also made use of a huge variety of wild plants
around them, such as samphire, locally known as *samper*, a
plant recorded as growing abundantly on the Isle of Wight
as far back as 1657.

Rock samphire, considered the best variety, grew on
cliff faces across the Island, especially around Freshwater
and the Needles, whilst golden samphire, a good second
best, could be found in salt marshes along the Medina and
at Newtown. Both of these varieties have a similar salty
flavour but are actually different to the samphire sold in
UK supermarkets today. Instead, this version is a species of
marsh samphire or glasswort which could also be found on
the Island's riverbanks but there's little evidence that locals
held it in much esteem.

Rock samphire was collected by *cliffsmen* who tied

baskets round their waist, drove a crowbar into the brow of a cliff, attached a rope and then lowered themselves down to the crevices where the samphire grew. In some cases men died or injured themselves gathering it, the danger naturally making it more expensive. With the difference in price, it wasn't uncommon for samphire dealers to try and pass off the easily gathered golden samphire as the prestigious cliff face variety, and with uninitiated customers they would often succeed.

Islanders minced up the samphire and served it with melted butter - supposedly a good substitute for the caper sauce used to accompany fish - and also created a warm, aromatic samphire pickle which was a common feature on Island tables. This wasn't only made on the Isle of Wight as large quantities of samphire were collected at Freshwater, put in barrels of sea water and sent to the wholesale houses in London who made it to their own recipes.

Aside from this, other edible coastal plants included sea rocket, sea radish and wild asparagus, as well as wild cabbage - which seemed to disappear from the Island by 1900 - and sea kale, whose blue-green leaves can still be seen on local beaches today.

Some of the rarer wild species could be found growing at Ryde, on a sandy turf-covered area by the sea known as the *duver* (also spelt 'dover' - and a rival to the one at St. Helens). Here, some of the Island's rarest plants could thrive, as did a number which escaped from nearby cottage gardens.

By 1860, the *duver* had almost entirely disappeared under the newly built houses of The Strand, but before that time, among the grasses, gorse and rushes, locals could find horseradish, wild celery, black mustard and marsh mallow growing in its sandy soil.

A number of species were also used by people on the Isle of Wight as a substitute for spinach, including *assmirt*, the hot leaves of the water pepper plant. Similarly, some of the poorer Islanders would gather the young leaves of sea beet - a plant from the same family as chard and beetroot, which grew on a number of rocky shorelines. It was known to them as *wild spinage* or *beet* and was boiled and eaten with pork or bacon.

In terms of salad leaves, watercress was the plant of choice for local people but land cress also made a good substitute. In 1856, a local botanist remarked that land cress was generally thought to have been introduced to Europe from North America but 'be that as it may, no plant is more thoroughly naturalised amongst us… and in no part of Britain perhaps does it abound more than in this island'. Land cress was also known to Islanders as *bank cress*, a name which, according to the English Dialect Dictionary, was used on the Isle of Wight and nowhere else in the whole country.

Other useful species included white, black and hedge mustard, wild fennel, lamb's lettuce and chicory, wild garlic (especially favoured by the local Romani gypsy minority), common mallow (whose seeds were known as *cheeses*) and angelica (whose crystallised stems are often used in desserts).

As time progressed, knowledge of some wild plants disappeared and their usage died out. Alexanders (*smyrnium olusatrum*), a native of the Mediterranean which was introduced to Britain many centuries ago, may have been one of the first to become forgotten on the Isle of Wight. The stems could be eaten raw, having a similar taste and texture to celery, and the rest of the plant could be boiled and eaten as a leaf vegetable.

During the Tudor period, alexanders were highly esteemed and commonly cultivated in kitchen gardens, as their presence growing wild in some of the oldest inhabited parts of the Island seems to indicate. In the 19th century they could be found at Brighstone, Brading and close to the crumbling ruins of Carisbrooke Castle, Quarr and the Seamark church at St. Helens. However, alexanders had already been 'quite forgotten' and had outlived 'all record of its use in the Isle of Wight', being replaced by cultivated celery which was grown in almost every garden.

Herbs were also an important part of Isle of Wight cooking. Thyme, marjoram and horehound were all common on the chalky hills and sheep walks of the Downs, as was salad burnet, a plant whose slender leaves taste like cucumber. In woodlands and thickets you could find chervil, herb bennet, wild basil and wood sorrel, while meadowsweet grew by the banks of streams and rivers.

Wild chamomile was quite rare on the Island but common chamomile was abundant on a number of heaths and commons, including St. Helens Green; and wild mint grew in many places, quite likely being used to make the homemade mint flavoured sweets known as *bull's eyes*.

Some of these herbs were also planted in cottage gardens, and non-native bay, borage, sage, parsley and rosemary grew well on the Island too, with the latter having a special cultural significance for local people.

On the Isle of Wight, as in other regions, rosemary was associated with remembrance and was used in the traditions and practices that marked the end of someone's life. The custom of scattering rosemary into the grave was common on the Island and the ancient tradition of people in a funeral procession carrying sprigs of rosemary was retained at Yarmouth into the 19th century.

Besides these rituals, the herb was also used in the baking of a special 'cake' to mark the occasion. When the writer Hubert Garle made his driving tour of the Island at the start of the 20th century, he came across a funeral at Shorwell and described how the guests afterwards returned home to eat cakes flavoured with rosemary. The tradition didn't end there, as on the following day it was usual to send 'half a dozen of these cakes, wrapped in a white cloth, to the clergyman, as a memento of the deceased'.

There's little information to tell us exactly what these cakes were like and it's possible we'll never really know but it seems they sometimes contained spices and were probably fairly small, round and flavoured with freshly chopped rosemary.

"The hogs are of a breed,
I believe, peculiar to the
island; at least I do not
recollect seeing any of
the same in other places.
They are large and tall,
marked with black spots,
and have very deep sides;
their bacon is excellent"

Meat

There's no doubt that meat was an important part in the diet of many people on the Isle of Wight, especially pork, lamb and mutton, which were key components in the local style of cookery.

Fried pork was one of the most common meals for many Islanders, often eaten with cabbage, turnip greens or sometimes with sea beet. Pork steaks were known as *grisken* and the jaw was called a *choppekin* - a cut that was usually smoked and salted, possibly using local sea salt from the salterns of Newtown or Seaview.

Butchers made a *chine* from the neck, being scored and salted, maybe even stuffed with herbs as it is in Lincolnshire. Smoked hams, sausages, black pudding and bacon were also made; with little going to waste, even the heart and liver were used in the kitchen.

Many farms across the Island kept pigs and they were especially profitable for coastal farmers who could take them onto the beaches at low tide to eat the sand hoppers - a small, nutritious crustacean, which the pigs were said to greatly enjoy.

At one point in time - around the late Georgian period - it

seems the Isle of Wight might have even had its own breed of pig, described as tall, spotted and providing excellent bacon. Years later, the Berkshire and Sussex breed of pig would increasingly be used by local farmers meaning that the Island's own breed became much rarer and would eventually disappear altogether.

Isle of Wight lamb was considered some of the best in the country and local mutton was a common feature in many Islanders' cooking. Tens of thousands of sheep grazed on the Downs and up to five thousand lambs were sent to London butchers in a single year. Many were pure Dorset or Southdown sheep while others were crossed with the Somerset breed.

Their meat was eaten all year round but took on an especially important role in the celebration of *hooam harvest*, when the last of the wheat or barley had been gathered at the end of the summer. All the farm workers and house servants were invited to eat with the master and his family, with a leg of mutton or mutton pies often taking pride of place for the first course, along with a ham or a chine.

Whilst pork and lamb were commonplace, beef started out as a rare feature on Isle of Wight tables. If you wanted good quality beef, people believed it had to come from cattle bred exclusively for their meat. However, almost all cattle on the Island were dairy cows, especially after the Island started to develop a reputation for the quality of its milk, cream and butter.

Back in 1754, when the author Henry Fielding visited Ryde, the local butcher only supplied beef a few times a year whilst mutton was available all year round. The arrival of fresh, new beef was often an exciting event accompanied with a certain level of showmanship, such as when Newport's main butcher would go to Salisbury every December to bring back a fat oxen, 'bedecked with ribbons' refusing to sell the meat to anyone but his loyal, year-round customers.

By the mid-19th century beef was becoming more common, with excellent quality, locally reared meat appearing on butchers' counters all year round, however it still kept an association with being a meat for special occasions - especially Christmas.

In 1871, ten sailors from the *Iron Duke* found themselves stuck on the Island over the festive period after being wrongfully accused of disobedience. When the court case collapsed the people of Ryde tried to make the sailors as comfortable as possible, providing them with a Christmas dinner of roast beef and plum pudding.

One of these sailors was Dutch and three others were black men from Canada, the U.S.A. and Jamaica, and it's nice to think that their first taste of Isle of Wight hospitality was being treated to the best festive meal that the Island had to offer.

From the mid-19th century, Islanders also began to have turkey on Christmas Day, including locally bred birds from the 1880s. Mark Hooper, a fishmonger of Pier Street in Ryde became renowned for his 'inexhaustible' displays of turkey, goose and game at Christmas time, including prize winning turkeys that weighed over 200lbs.

Throughout the rest of the year, people on the Island also ate hares, rabbits, pheasants, partridges, wild ducks such as teal, wild geese and wood pigeons (locally called *wood quest* or *wood quester*).

Chickens were readily available, supplying local people as well as the military and ships anchored off Cowes and St. Helens. Deer lived in Parkhurst Forest at the end of the 18th century and were kept on a few estates such as Appuldurcombe, meaning that venison may have also made an appearance on upper class menus from time to time.

Whilst meat was important to many on the Island, there were vegetarians too, even in the 18th and 19th centuries. One in particular attracted a lot of attention: Judith Banister, who died at Cowes in 1754, aged 108, after apparently living on just biscuits, apples, milk and water for the last sixty years of her life.

"The prawns pay best. They are taken in large numbers, and sent off cooked, hot from the pot, to London fish-dealers, who, in the early season, pay as much as 10s. or 12s. per hundred."

Fish

Seafood was a core component of Isle of Wight cooking and many generations of Islanders earned a living from work on the seas. The different species of fish and shellfish living in the Island's waters were unlike those in many other parts of the country, providing another element that would have made its regional cuisine distinctive.

Crabs and lobsters were found on the Island's south coast in great numbers and 'of uncommon size and excellence', employing up to twenty fishermen from every coastal village in their collection. Niton in particular was a focal point for crab and lobster fishing and was even known for many years by the name Crab Niton.

They were caught in circular woven pots made by local fishermen, using the young stems of willow, known as *withies*. The willow was grown in plantations called *withy beds* which could be found on the edges of many South Wight villages, such as Brook and Bonchurch.

Prawns were abundant in this area too and could even be gathered by hand in shallow waters. Known as *prankles* in the local dialect, they were taken in large numbers from rocky parts of the coastline and 'sent off cooked, hot from the pot, to London fish-dealers'.

The Island also had a reputation for its shrimps - a fact mentioned by Mrs. Beeton in her *Book of Household Management*. They were generally potted which involved cooking the shrimps in lots of melted butter and spices before pouring the mixture into small ceramic pots to cool, the butter setting and acting as a preservative.

Native oysters naturally occured in the Solent, Medina and Newtown Creek. Said to be small but with a 'superior flavour' they have been eaten by locals for many centuries. Vast oyster beds used to stretch from the Island to Portsmouth, Southampton and Hayling Island but were dredged so unsustainably that young oysters from the waters around Jersey had to be brought in to revive the population.

Many men from Cowes specialised in oyster fishing in the Solent, with Osborne Bay a favoured spot to find them. If the oysters were too small, they were stored in oyster ponds to mature, and if they were large enough they were sold locally to pubs and fish markets.

Interestingly, The Folly Inn, on the River Medina, actually started life in the Georgian period as a barge known for its lively oyster banquets. By the 1790s it had been hauled up onto the shore and converted into a pub, with the forecastle being turned into a parlour and parts of the stern made into a kitchen and cellar.

The owner was called 'the Oystericus of Newport', a man who would annually line the bottom of the Medina with young oysters brought over from Cancale in France - a region known as the oyster capital of Brittany. Once they had matured, these oysters were harvested and used to supply the shellfish banquets which took place at The Folly for many decades thereafter.

From the mid-19th century, oyster farming on the Isle of

Wight became much more commercialised, with fisheries being established in the Medina, Brading Haven, Newtown and Fishbourne - though they each had mixed fortunes.

Newtown Creek was one of the smallest and despite the fact that ninety-five thousand oysters were supplied from its waters in just one seven-month period, the fishery's owners struggled to make it profitable in the long-term.

Brading Haven on the other hand had better chances as it was larger and had been noted for the quality of its oysters since the 1790s. In 1873, Major Boyle started to commercialise oyster fishing in the area but only three years into the scheme he was forced to give up his new oyster beds as Bembridge Embankment was being built and the Haven was about to be drained.

Possibly the most successful was The Medina River Oyster Company who brought young oysters from the Solent, France and Portugal to lay down in the Medina to mature. They were said to have a delicate flavour which was apparently highly esteemed by the French.

Aside from oysters, many tons of scallops and winkles were also gathered, much being sent to London, and Isle of Wight cockles were renowned for their quality and nutritious properties. However, local superstition meant that some other species of shellfish were originally avoided by some Islanders.

In 1795, Richard Warner remarked in his *History of the Isle of Wight* that mussels were never cooked in the area as people believed them to be harmful or even poisonous. Limpets too were ignored because of the difficulty in removing them from the rocks and the fact that razor clams are edible seemed unknown to many. Warner wrote: 'I believe the Islanders are unacquainted with the excellence of this fish; since I did not find that they ever made a practice of taking them'. By the 1830s though, things had begun to change and most locally occurring shellfish such as these could be bought from Isle of Wight fishmongers.

Saltwater fish were also a key part of the Island's regional cooking with two particularly small species especially favoured by local people.

The first was the thin, silvery sand eel or sand lance which lived close to a number of the Island's sandy shorelines but was especially associated with Sandown Bay where they seemed to thrive. Known locally as *sand sprats*, they were considered 'excellent eating' so fishermen devoted a lot of time and effort to obtain them.

As the tide went out, the sand lances could be found burrowing into the sand, fourteen inches below the surface and by using a fork or spade they could easily be turned up and caught. Great numbers of *sprats* were gathered in this way and sold by the quart, although in later years nets were used too. A guide to Sandown from 1867 described the fish as 'somewhat similar to whitebait' and explained that lodging house keepers in the town knew how to cook them to perfection.

Another local favourite were sand smelts, a small migratory fish commonly found swimming in shoals close to the shore on the north side of the Island. Up until the 1900s, fishermen would go to Cowes Esplanade and the nearby quays and piers every day to catch sand smelts using their drop nets. These finely meshed nets were stretched over an iron hoop and lowered gently below the surface of the water by a pole. Smelts react swiftly, so as soon as they swam over the top of the net, it was quickly brought up to catch them. Tourists too would occasionally take part and in the 1830s some of the lodging houses at Cowes that backed onto the sea allowed their guests to procure sand smelts 'by their own prowess'.

Other than these, the most common sea fish included pollock (locally called *whiting cole*), plaice, bass, flounder, mullet, sole and pouting. Mackerel appeared off the south coast in the summer months, with a small and especially sweet variety known as 'Chale Bay Mackerel' being especially sought after. Dogfish (known as *suss* or *peak hound*) was also eaten and brown trout was commonly found swimming in the Island's freshwater streams.

Huge numbers of eels were caught, both at sea and in rivers, including conger eels and the now critically endangered European eel. Local legend says that Shepherd's Chine, near Atherfield, actually got its name after a shepherd diverted a stream running into Cowleaze Chine to get to the eels that lived on the riverbed below. He was planning to restore the stream back to its original course afterwards but heavy rains deepened the new channel so much it became impossible, the water eventually forming a new ravine, known from then on as Shepherd's Chine.

Pilchards, on the other hand - a fish more commonly associated with Cornwall - were only occasional visitors to Island waters, as were ling, dab and John Dories. Herrings, traditionally eaten with barley bread and cheese by Quarr Abbey's harvest workers, seem to become much less common during the 19th century and species such as salmon and hake were so rare they were almost never caught by local fishermen.

Much of what was written about Isle of Wight fish was penned by visiting authors who may have been unaware of the traditional ways of cooking fish that Islanders could have practiced in their own homes.

It's likely many were boiled in fish kettles or simply fried in butter and as *sand sprats* were compared with whitebait, they may have been dusted in flour and deep fried. Cabbage, sea beet or watercress could have been served alongside, as well as the chopped up rock samphire and melted butter mixture, mentioned by the local botanist William Arnold Bromfield. No doubt Islanders cooked their seafood in many more interesting and unusual ways but as so little was written down, they may be lost forever.

"There was a pleasant restfulness about the dairy on a market day, the shelves of fresh-made butter, the result of long and heavy labour, each pat wrapped in cool green dock leaves"

Cheese

During the 19th century, the Island was famed for the quality of its dairy products. A combination of lush grazing and carefully bred cattle combined to create some of the finest milk in the country. Island farmers brought over the best milking cows to improve their herds including Devons and Alderneys as well as some Guernsey and Welsh cattle too.

The result was a much richer butter than that which was made from 'the English cow' and some cows could produce enough milk to make up to nine or ten pounds of butter a week. Even the smallest farms on the Isle of Wight had a dairy where butter was made using a churn called a *plumper* - the process of churning being known as *plumping* (a word also used in the West Country). Once the milk had turned to butter, it was cut and shaped, with the newly formed pats often being wrapped in dock leaves to keep them fresh.

The fame of the Island's butter wasn't only known locally. When the American author of *The Last of the Mohicans* - James Fenimore Cooper - landed at Cowes in the 1820s, he was already well aware that the Isle of Wight was celebrated for the quality of its butter. Although, being accustomed to added salt back in America, it took him a while to get used to it.

A cheese-making culture also existed on the Island however it wasn't always so well understood by outside observers. An object of particular fascination was the *Chock Dog* or *Isle of Wight Rock*, names given to a hard cheese produced on the Island using the leftover skimmed milk created during the cream and butter making processes. It was a much firmer cheese and the longer it was kept the harder and dryer it became.

Writers joked that you needed firm teeth and a strong stomach to try it and that you might have to use an axe or a saw to cut into it. Newspapers around the country printed a story about an Isle of Wight cheese in America - the recipient managing to kill himself and his son when his knife slipped trying to cut the cheese open. Another story described how some Isle of Wight cheeses were sent to London for the Great Exhibition of 1851 where they were incorrectly labelled as 'Isle of Wight grindstones'.

This Isle of Wight cheese was certainly unusual and it's true that sometimes it was hard enough to be rolled home with a stick, however a significant quantity was produced by Island dairies and a substantial amount of it was eaten on the Island.

Not only that, but there is evidence it was valued amongst local people too. When Afton Farm and its contents were sold at auction in 1834, amongst the lots of 'Household Furniture' was one for 'Isle of Wight cheese and pickled pork'. Local shops were also keen to sell it. Benjamin Lower of The Assam Tea Warehouse in Newport High Street put an advert in the *Hampshire Advertiser* with the line: 'Wanted, a few dairies of good Isle of Wight Cheese'.

What seems most likely is that the hard Isle of Wight

cheese was considered unusual from an outsider's perspective and didn't fit with the popular tastes of the time. These days, other hard cheeses made from skimmed milk (such as Parmesan and Monterey Jack) are much more commonly eaten and better appreciated.

Despite all the attention being focused on the Island's hard skimmed milk cheese, other varieties were created in smaller quantities as well. The best kind of cheese was known as *rammel cheese* and was made from fresh, whole milk.

Island people were also well acquainted with blue cheese which was locally called *blue vinnid* or *vinney* (a name said to come from the Old English word *fynig*). It's likely much of this was imported from Dorset but it's possible Island dairy farmers made it too - and considering the richness of the Island milk it would have no doubt been very good.

'No one in the world has tasted junket as these island people make it'

Sweets & Desserts

In the past, Islanders made a variety of cakes, pastries, sweets and puddings, ranging from the crude mint flavoured sweets called *bull's eyes* to the internationally recognised *Isle of Wight Cracknels* - and luckily a lot of information about them still exists.

Doughnuts (also simply called *nuts*) were made on the Island for many hundreds of years. Despite sharing a name with the American doughnut (which has Dutch origins), it seems that the Isle of Wight version developed completely independently from their Atlantic cousins, with some claiming that they can be traced as far back as the 17th century.

One key difference with the Isle of Wight Doughnut is the filling - historically it would have been small, wild plums but sometimes currants were used instead. An early recipe also includes an interesting combination of spices in the dough - allspice, cinnamon, cloves and mace. Some of these are grown in the Caribbean, while others are sourced from Asia but considering the importance of Cowes as an international shipping port and customs depot during the 18th and early 19th centuries, it's not hard to see how

Islanders could have got hold of these far-flung ingredients.

In their earliest years, Isle of Wight Doughnuts were also known as *bird's nests* - a name which came about from their appearance when cut in half with the cluster of plums in the middle. They were produced in homes and bakeries across the Island but were little known in the rest of the UK at the time, travel writers having to explain to their readers exactly what they were. Rosa Raine noted in her book 'Now I fancy you wondering what a doughnut can be; you never tasted one, if this is your first visit here; for doughnuts are peculiar to the Island'.

A recipe from 1845 describes how flour, milk, lard, yeast, spices and fine brown sugar are combined to make the dough which is then left to rise by the fire. Once kneaded, the mixture is formed into doughnuts about the size of a cricket ball, a hole is made with the thumb and the filling is inserted. Then the raw doughnuts are thrown into boiling lard until golden and traditionally drained on clean straw.

Doughnuts were eaten all year round but they were especially associated with Shrove Tuesday. Children known as *shrovers* would knock on doors in their neighbourhood and sing a song which included the lines:

'A piece of bread, a piece of cheese
A bit of your fat beyacun
Or a dish of doughnuts
Aal of your own meyacun!'

Aside from doughnuts, Islanders created a wide variety of other cakes, pastries and desserts, often involving fruit. Plum cake, raspberry tarts, *apple pudden* and gooseberry tarts were regularly made, as was *apple stucklen* - a small, thin and semi-circular pastry eaten by labourers in the fields at harvest time. Similar to an apple turnover, *stucklens* were made by folding sliced apples and sugar inside a rough pastry and baking without a tin or dish.

Some cakes were only made at specific times of year that had a special seasonal or spiritual significance. *Hollan cakes* were made for the fast of All Hallow's Eve (also known as Hollantide, 31st October) and *Hallan cakes* were made for All Saint's Day (Hallantide, 1st November). On Shrove Tuesday, small flat cakes known as *shrove cakes* were prepared, at harvest time seed cakes were baked and *figgy pudden* was made for Christmas.

Other sweets included *vlitters* - a small pancake which most likely resembled drop scones or Welsh *crempog* pancakes - and *flick cake* which instead of looking like a sponge had the texture of flaky pastry. This unusual consistency was made by replacing butter or lard with the leaf fat from the inside of the pig - known locally as *flick* or *vlick*.

Islanders also made puddings with their rich and creamy dairy products, including a special dessert mentioned by two 19th century writers that became something of an Isle of Wight speciality.

During his tour of the Island in the 1840s, the British author George Mogridge visited a thatched cottage in Binstead that stood amongst trees in the hollow of an old stone quarry. He described it as 'one of the prettiest little snuggeries' that you could possibly imagine and praised their basins of 'curd and whey'.

Around the same time, over in Freshwater, a three year old girl celebrated her birthday with a feast laid out on a low haystack in the barnyard of a farmhouse. There was cake, Isle of Wight doughnuts but also 'Isle of Wight junket'. Remembering this party many years later, the author, Edith Nicholl Ellison mentions that 'no one in the world has tasted junket as these island people make it'. She explains: it's a superior type of clabber (a firm, milky yoghurt), covered an inch deep in thick yellow cream and scattered with 'Hundreds and Thousands' - which at the time were just red and blue in colour.

The 'curd and whey' of Mogridge and the 'junket' of Ellison are both in fact the same thing - an ancient milk-based dessert, similar to a panna cotta, which can be traced back to the medieval period. The word is said to originate from Old French *jonquette*, similar to the Italian *giuncata*, meaning a cream cheese dish served in or drained through a rush basket.

Junkets are often flavoured with brandy (but sometimes rosewater or orange blossom are used instead) and they have remained strongly associated with the West Country, especially Devon, where they've been popular for centuries. However, it seems the Isle of Wight made their own versions of this dessert and developed a reputation for them too.

Finally, the Isle of Wight was also noted for its biscuits. In the 18th century, considerable quantities of *naval biscuits* were made at Hurst Stake Mill on the River Medina to supply the Royal Navy at Portsmouth and another type of biscuit became one of the Island's most famous creations - the *Isle of Wight Cracknel*, a biscuit whose full story will be told in the next chapter.

"The Cracknels... must then be taken out, and plunged in cold water to harden; after which, they are to be slowly dried, washed over with well beaten whites of eggs, and baked on tin plates, in an oven sufficiently brisk to make them crisp, but not by any means high coloured"

Isle of Wight Cracknels

The Isle of Wight Cracknel (sometimes also spelt cracknell) was a sweet biscuit, lightly flavoured with nutmeg and rose water, that was boiled before being brushed with egg white and baked. It became incredibly popular during the early Victorian period and could have been considered the Island's most famous culinary export.

There were other types of biscuits also called cracknels, the name said to come from the French word *craquelin*, meaning 'a hard brittle cake', however, the Isle of Wight version had a long history and was considered unique and different - even at the time.

The origin of the Isle of Wight Cracknel is still pretty mysterious though. Supposedly King George III (who ruled from 1760 to 1820) was sent a box of them every year and by 1830 a factory in Cowes had a board outside describing itself as the 'Old Established Cracknel Manufactory' - suggesting it had been in business for a long time already.

Although cracknels were made all over the Island, Cowes certainly seems to have been their birthplace and the factory, located in Bath Road, was possibly the first place they were made on any big scale, being run throughout the

1840s and 1850s by a local man named Charles Pinhorn.

Apart from the Island market, these biscuits were also sent in large quantities to the mainland. By the middle of the 19th century, Isle of Wight Cracknels could be found right across the United Kingdom at grocers in Worcester, Norwich, Wolverhampton, Colchester and Devizes. Shops on Oxford Street in London announced them as 'fresh from the Isle of Wight daily', George Lugton of Dublin sold them in his 'Italian warehouse' and W. Bremner, a druggist from Thurso in northern Scotland, put an advert in the *John O'Groat Journal* to say he still had a few boxes left for sale.

However, by this point in time Isle of Wight Cracknels had started to be manufactured on the mainland too. Whether the original recipe hadn't been kept secret or whether the process was easy enough to guess, these biscuits were no longer baked exclusively on the Island.

Recipes for them appeared in cookbooks from 1839 and 1851 enabling companies such as Hill's of Bishopsgate in London, Pursell's of Regent Street and The Liverpool Steam Biscuit Factory to make their own and market them as Isle of Wight Cracknels. Some of these businesses even promoted cracknels as their star product, publishing adverts with titles such as 'Hill's Celebrated Isle of Wight Cracknells for Coffee, Dessert or Ice', clearly confident their customers wouldn't be put off by these Island specialities being made outside their home region.

Although the Isle of Wight Cracknel was becoming separated from its origins, the big companies of London and Liverpool were actually helping to turn this biscuit into a household name, not just in the UK but overseas too. By 1850, Hill & Jones, an export biscuit baker based in Jewry Street, London was offering their Isle of Wight Cracknels to 'regimental messes and private families' living in India and other parts of the Empire.

They clearly had an international appeal, at least in areas of British influence, as we can even find references that show they were being manufactured abroad. In 1845, Thomas Holmes of Hobart, Tasmania was baking them and selling them for 1s. 6d. per pound, but perhaps the most intriguing example is W. L. Atkinson & Co. based in Old Court House Street, Calcutta. Founded by a British family who had lived in India for generations, they described their Isle of Wight Cracknels as 'a favourite ladies' biscuit' and sold them loose at 10 Annas per pound, or at 2 Rupees for a three pound tin.

In the same way that these biscuits have unclear origins, their demise is also difficult to chart. The 1850s seem to have been the height of their popularity but pretty soon afterwards all mention of them disappears.

One of the last references comes from 1878 when The Original Hastings Biscuit Shop in Sussex still advertised their homemade Isle of Wight Cracknels but soon after they must have fallen into obscurity. Whether it was because they fell out of favour or because they had become so separated from their Isle of Wight origin that they took on another name is hard to tell - and we'll probably never really know.

"It is brewing day,
and the farmer, in a
white smock with the
sleeves turned up to
the elbows, is very busy
superintending the brew,
and carrying pails of
water to the large copper
already enveloped in
clouds of steam"

Drink

Alcohol has been made on the Isle of Wight since ancient times and the local drinking culture would have been an important part of Island identity. For hundreds of years, locally occurring ingredients were brewed or fermented to make alcoholic drinks and fruits often used to flavour spirits. Alcohol wasn't only important socially but also played a significant role in a number of local traditions and ceremonies.

Spirits like gin and brandy were especially popular amongst Islanders of the 18th and early 19th centuries. They were cheap and freely available, as most of it was supplied by the immense amounts of illegal smuggling that took place at the time.

Some of these spirits were brought over by secret sailing expeditions to France and landed in quiet bays at the Back of the Island, and some were carried ashore at Ryde hidden in the ship's washing. If barrels of alcohol became washed up from shipwrecks they were similarly whisked away and made good use of by local people.

Every level of Island society was said to be connected with smuggling, from the sailors and fisherman who did the hard work, to the gentry who were the main customers. Whole villages, like Niton, were involved in the trade and few Islanders could see much harm in what they were doing.

In order to disguise this smuggled alcohol from the authorities, the local custom of infusing spirits with fruits came in useful - often mixing gin or brandy with cherries or sloes. It was even suggested that the long since demolished hamlet of Cherrygin, near Appley, took its name from this practice (although other sources disagree).

It's likely the Island also had a much older tradition of making fruit wines and liqueurs, which a few drops of spirits helped to enhance and preserve. In the mid-19th century, elderberries would be gathered every autumn from gardens and hedgerows to turn into elderberry wine, a winter drink that would make a rich and fruity mulled wine at Christmas.

A story was also told of a kind, elderly couple who lived in the centre of Ryde and were famed for their wines made from the fruit of the gooseberry and currant bushes that grew in their garden. They would never sell their fruit to anyone and instead turned it all into wine and jams which were highly esteemed by their select circle of friends.

The small, sour grapes which grew on cottage garden vines were also used to make wine, as were rhubarb and wild flowers. During the height of spring, local people would set off with large baskets to the Downs to collect cowslips to make into a much admired cowslip wine. It's likely gillyflowers (locally called *gillafers*) which grew in gardens and wild on the cliffs were used to infuse alcoholic drinks too. We know local people gathered them from the cliff edges, some badly injuring themselves in the process.

Not all spirits were mixed with flowers and fruit though. At Niton in the 1830s, gin was served hot, sweet and strong; and fiery brandy was mixed with beer to create a drink known as *dog's nose*. On special occasions such as a birth or wedding, *egg flip* would be concocted. To make it, two quarts of ale were heated over a fire with half a pint of brandy and a dozen beaten eggs mixed in. The whole thing would be stirred until it boiled and after a minute or two would then be poured into an earthenware jug and served hot.

Brewing also took place on a large scale using locally grown barley and wild hops which could be found in woods across the Island.

Beer came in a variety of forms, including *swizzle* (a light version made from ale and beer mixed together) and *nammet beer* (the strongest type, carried out to harvest workers in a small keg called a puncheon).

Ale, locally called *eal* or *yeal* also has a long history and took on special significance in the ancient wassailing tradition that was continued at Yarmouth for many centuries. It was a drinking ritual that took place on New Year's Day when a wooden bowl of mulled ale was taken from house to house and participants would sing a wassail song, wishing health to the town for the coming year.

Similarly, cider held an important place in the Island's drinking culture. Most farmers made from two to six hogsheads of cider every year, mostly for themselves but its excellent quality meant people in Hampshire were prepared to offer high prices to Island farmers if they'd sell a part of their annual produce. Some of the Island's cider makers may have also used the local variety of apple - The Isle of Wight Pippin - which was said to be a 'valuable' cider fruit and may have produced a distinctive or unusual flavour. Whatever variety was used, Hampshire people held Isle of Wight cider in high estimation but despite having many apple trees around them, made relatively little themselves.

Aside from apples and barley, Islanders may also have fermented honey to create the ancient drink mead. Little information exists, but we can find one brief glimpse from 1820 when the Irish novelist Marguerite Blessington made her tour of the Island. On her way to Wootton from East Cowes, she met an elderly woman carrying a pot of honey. The writer explains: 'she wished me very much to taste the honey, apparently from pure good nature and civility, and gave us a little history of her having consumed the rest of her luscious store in making mead'. A truly ancient drink, it's possible that even by this time the custom of making it on the Island was falling into disuse.

Minority Food Cultures on the Isle of Wight

Of course it wasn't only white British Islanders who lived and cooked on the Isle of Wight - there were others who they shared the landscape with, bringing their own culinary traditions and cultural connections with them.

The Island's gypsy minority certainly had a distinctive food culture which at times overlapped with that of other Islanders. These travellers came from a mixed variety of backgrounds but many were ethnically Romani and made their money from a number of trades including selling buttons, pegs and basketwork.

Living in tents or caravans, they camped at numerous locations across the Isle of Wight during the 19th century, including Alum Bay and St. Helens Green. Some were given permission by landowners to create more permanent settlements allowing encampments to remain for many years, such as those at Rowborough, near Brading and at Marks Corner on the edge of Parkhurst Forest.

The gypsies cooked over open fires and made good use of the wild food that was available to them on the Island. We know they caught and ate rabbits, and it seems they made good money supplying them to other Islanders too. Turnip greens and watercress were also used in their cooking, as well as wild garlic - a plant not frequently used by others on the Island.

Writing for *The Phytologist* magazine in 1842, local botanist William Arnold Bromfield explained that a few years previously gypsy encampments had been common across the county and wild garlic was known to be a plant that featured in the gypsies' 'strong diets'. As a result, wild garlic - which was traditionally called *ramsons* - had also become known on the Island by the name of *gipsy onion*. To be influencing the local dialect, it seems the cultural traditions of this community had clearly made a significant impression on the rest of the Island's population.

South Asians were another minority whose food culture made a mark on Island history. It is now a well known fact that during the late 19th century, Queen Victoria had chicken curry prepared for her most Sundays while she stayed at Osborne House. Her Indian cooks Ghulam Mustafa and Sheikh Chidda prepared these curries, based more closely on Anglo-Indian than authentically Indian traditions, and may well have used ingredients from the house's own model farm at Barton Manor.

It's also possible that the Asian sailors who briefly lived on the Island during the 1840s and 1850s maintained their own culinary traditions and we know Asian cooks worked on a number of ships that visited the Island during the First World War. As these boats were largely crewed by *lascar* sailors who came from the Indian subcontinent, cooks of the same background were often employed to cater for them.

Noor Mahommed prepared meals on board *H.M.T. Inventor* which docked at Cowes in 1915 and chief cook Wasta Gomez was employed on the *Matheren* which visited the Island in 1916. Gomez was a Roman Catholic who came from a historically Portuguese area of India. The food of his home region included flavours and influences from Portugal and these may well have made an impression on the meals he cooked on ship. Sadly, whilst his vessel was moored in the Solent, Gomez suffered a brain haemorrhage and died, being buried at Northwood Cemetery shortly afterwards.

The small African and Caribbean minority who lived on the Island may also have retained some of the practices and customs of their homelands and the numerous inter-racial relationships also provided an opportunity for cultural crossover.

A number of black servants worked for wealthy families living on the Island during the 18th and 19th centuries, many of whom were unlikely to have had any formal instruction in cooking. Some domestic cooks, such as the Jamaican-born Fanny Eaton, came to the profession later in life. Eaton had been an artists' model in her twenties and thirties but by 1901 was working as a cook for John D. Hall, a Hammersmith wine merchant at his home in Alexandra Road, Ryde.

Not only is it possible that these cooks and servants may have retained some of the influences of their home countries but they may have been actively encouraged to do so. In Georgian Britain, West Indian food and drink such as pineapple, guava and rum punch were the height of fashion and some of their employers were retired naval captains and administrators who had spent years working in the Caribbean and were well acquainted with its food culture.

Finally, it's likely the Island's historic Jewish community also maintained their culinary customs, especially around religious ceremonies which often require a *seudah* - an obligatory festive meal. For example, after the birth of Isaac, son of Judah Lima Cohen, at Cowes in 1778 it's possible that amongst other things, the family made a braided *challah* loaf - and they may have even used Isle of Wight flour to make it.

Although much of the food culture of the Isle of Wight's minorities is hard to rediscover, snapshots from some groups show how Islanders of different backgrounds also shared in the Island's landscape, potentially using local products in their traditional cuisines and even influencing other Islanders as well. Of course, many of these minorities were well integrated into Island society so it's also likely that they experienced traditional Isle of Wight food and may have even taken some elements to adapt and incorporate into their own style of cooking.

Later European Influences

Possibly the most exciting period for Isle of Wight food was during the late 19th century when new culinary trends from Europe were increasingly influencing what was eaten on the Island. Whilst ultimately new trends like these would lead to the demise of historic Isle of Wight food, for some decades these two completely different styles of cooking lived together side by side.

Even as far back as the 1850s, menus for the upper classes could include tongue rissoles, 'genuine' turtle soup and oyster chowder. Some bakers on the Island started producing German biscuits, Vienna bread and Italian macaroons alongside their local products and confectionary shops began to sell coloured French sweets.

Encouraging these trends more than anything was the Island's new status as a fashionable place to live - especially after Queen Victoria made Osborne House her summer retreat.

It attracted wealthy families to move to the Island from across the world including Polish-born Major General Rudolphe Zelaziewitch and retired Turkish-Greek banker Michael Spartali. Inevitably they each had their own tastes and many were used to the types of fine dining that were current in London or Paris.

Furthermore, the catering for these families was increasingly undertaken by European professionals. Many of these wealthy residents only lived on the Island for part of the year so rather than temporarily employ local cooks, they brought their skilled catering staff with them. This included everyone from the Queen, who brought French chefs such as Alphonse Gouffe and Octave Raugeaus, to the German-American Landsby family who owned a house in Priory Road, Shanklin and employed a Belgian cook named Elie Constance.

Likewise, some British Islanders who returned from work abroad also brought back foreign servants, such as Mr Johnson of West Street, Ryde who returned from Russia with Navara Rablukova as a domestic cook for his family.

This phenomenon continued as the 19th century progressed and meant that the Island's richest residents and visitors were gradually becoming more and more removed from the traditional food of the Isle of Wight.

However it wasn't only inside the home that cooking was changing. At the turn of the 20th century, local hotels were increasingly owned by European proprietors who brought new ideas with them from across the Channel.

In 1899, The Ocean Hotel in Sandown was opened by Polish-born entrepreneur Henry (Henryk) Lowenfeld - who also built The Apollo Theatre in London - and in 1902, Hollier's in Shanklin was under the ownership of Mr. Eugene Schmidtt, a native of Germany.

Yelf's Hotel in Union Street, Ryde, was also run by a German businessman - Julius Vogel - from 1903 to 1905 and The Royal Hotel in Ventnor was owned for many years by a well-respected Belgian hotelier, Hubert Cloots.

These European business owners imported the latest continental trends, especially around food and the art of hospitality. To provide the best service possible they employed highly skilled waiters and cooks from across Europe too.

In Ventnor, the Marine Hotel employed a French *chef de cuisine* and a Belgian kitchen porter, while at the Crab and Lobster Hotel in Grove Road worked two Austro-Hungarian waiters: John Stein from Bohemia and Antin Frenrees from Hungary.

Over at the Royal Hotel, staff included seven Germans, four Swiss and one Austrian who worked in roles which ranged from *cuisinier* to *pantry man*.

Professional waitering was still a relatively new occupation in Britain at the time and Europeans were considered the finest. Many hotel owners in Germany and Switzerland would send their sons abroad to improve their language skills and learn their trade - beginning at the very bottom.

Often these catering professionals would move from hotel to hotel in an apprentice style system hoping to eventually become a hotel owner themselves. It's possible that Island hoteliers like Schmidtt and Vogel had followed this route on their own journey to proprietor.

What's more, the many wealthy visitors to the Island came to expect this type of fine catering. As a contrast, the American businessman John Morgan Richards had a much more rustic experience when he stayed at Belinda Cottage on Ventnor Esplanade, where the landlady took a red hot block of iron from the fire and threw it into the tea urn to heat the water. 'We fairly jumped from our chairs' he would later recall. Clearly this wasn't the sophisticated type of experience visitors had come to anticipate when they took a trip to the Island.

It wasn't just hotel catering that European professionals influenced on the Isle of Wight, but the dining trends of the Island's rich and famous too. Hubert Cloots, a native of Limbourg, near Liège in Belgium took over the licence for The Royal Hotel in 1895. Cloots joined the local Masonic Lodge and hosted their banquets at the hotel 'in his usual elegant style'. With two other local businessmen, he also built the Pavillion on Ventnor Esplanade which would later hold grand masquerade balls which were noted for Cloots' 'high-class style for supper and refreshments'.

Similarly, important events would increasingly use the best continental-inspired caterers to supply their functions. Gunter's of Berkeley Square, London, were a firm favourite on the Island - a business first founded by an Italian named Domenico Negri, and which specialised in English, French and Italian confectionery.

They supplied the food for 'fashionable weddings' across the Island throughout the 19th century, including that of Princess Beatrice which featured *consomme printanier* and *côtelette de moutons chaudes* on the menu.

But Gunter's were most famous for their ices which they provided for Cowes Regatta in the 1840s. Ices came in different forms, some involved cream and were more like modern day ice cream whilst others were without any milk and were closer to a sorbet or granita.

Interestingly, this may have been one of the few European trends to be adopted more generally by Islanders at the time. By 1854, ices were being made locally and one Ryde confectioner even had their own ice well at Binstead. It's also a possibility that when Island sweetmakers created their own ices they adapted them to suit local tastes, perhaps even using locally abundant fruits such as cherries and sloes to provide the flavourings.

By the early 1900s, traditional Isle of Wight food was in rapid decline, caused in part by these new trends and fashions but also by modernisation and the increasing mobility of people to and from the Island. It's fate was perhaps inevitable but luckily records still survive to help us rediscover this lost part of Island history.

Isle of Wight Culinary Terms

Applestucklen - a small apple pie made by folding sliced apples and sugar into a rough pastry and baking without a dish or pan. Small, thin and probably semi-circular. Similar to an apple turnover.

Assmirt - water pepper (*polygonum hydropiper*), a peppery tasting plant, considered locally as a wild type of spinach

Bank Cress - land cress / American land cress (*barbarea verna*)

Barm - yeast

Base - sea bass

Bletters - small pancakes, fritters, also known as 'vlitters'

Blue Vinnid Cheese / Blue Vinney - blue cheese

Boughten Cake - a cake bought from a shop, instead of being made at home

Bren Cheese - bread and cheese, the bread often made from barley

Callards - the leaves and sprouts of an open variety of cabbage, closer to modern-day spring greens or kale

Cheeses - the seeds of the mallow (*malva sylvestris*) which used to be eaten by children

Chock Dog - a name for the hard, dry cheese made on the Island from skimmed milk, also known as 'Isle of Wight Rock'

Choppekin - the salted and smoked jaw of a pig

Crumplen - a small apple with a wrinkled rind

Dewbit - a piece of bread and cheese taken by labourers early in the morning at harvest time, while dew is on the grass, an hour or two before work.

Dog's Nose - beer and brandy mixed together and drunk cold

Dredge / Drudge - a flour dredger, a tin box with holes in the top to scatter flour

Eal / Yeal - ale

Figgy Pudden - a plum pudding / Christmas pudding

Flick Cake / Vlick Cake - a cake with the texture of flaky pastry, made with the leaf fat from inside a pig before it's been melted down to make lard

Fraail Basket - a basket made of rushes, used by labourers to carry their food

Fresh - to take refreshment

Gillafers - the gillyflower (*matthiola incana*)

Gipsy Onion - wild garlic (*allium ursinum*) also known as 'ramsons' / 'ramsden'

Goosegogs - gooseberries

Grisken - a pork steak

Hallan Cakes - cakes baked for All Saints' Day (Hallantide), 1st November

Hogails / Haghails - the fruit of the common hawthorn (*crataegus monogyna*)

Hollan Cakes - cakes made for the fast of All Hallow's Eve (Hollantide), 31st October

Hooam Harvest - a meal and celebration held on farms at the end of the harvest

Hurts / Harts - the mostly likely name for the bilberry. Records mention that bilberries were known by another name in the Island but don't specify what they were called. *Hurts, whorts* and *hart-berry* were used in Hampshire so offer the most likely answer.

Inyuns / Ineyuns - onions

Isle of Wight Cracknels - a type of biscuit, flavoured with nutmeg and rosewater, first boiled and then baked. Known since at least the reign of King George III

Isle of Wight Doughnuts - the traditional type of spiced doughnut made on the Island, usually with plums in the middle but sometimes currants were used instead. Also known as a 'nut'

Isle of Wight Junket - a thick milk-based dessert, similar to panna cotta, served with clotted cream on top

Isle of Wight Pippin - a variety of orange apple, supposedly first introduced from Normandy

Isle of Wight Pudding - a steamed pudding of uncertain origin, mentioned as early as 1870. One of the first recipes (from 1885) includes as ingredients: chopped apple, currants, suet, bread crumbs, sugar, grated nutmeg and candied citrus peel.

Isle of Wight Rock - a name for the hard, dry cheese made on the Island from skimmed milk, also known as 'Chock Dog'

Jack i' the Hedge - hedge mustard (*sisymbrium officinale*)

Jipper - any juice or syrup, such as of pies and puddings

Jorum - a large cup

Kissen Crusts - the name used if two loaves of bread have become stuck together while baking

Kix / Kecksy - the wild bullace or plum

Lintzeed - linseed

Mallus / Mash Mallus - the marsh mallow plant (*althaea officinalis*)

Merries - wild cherries (*prunus avium*) - from the French word *merise*

Merry Garden - cherry orchard

Nammet / Nammut - a lunch, eaten in the fields by farm labourers, usually at nine in the morning but at four in the afternoon during harvest time. Usually consists of bread, cheese and a strong 'nammet beer'

Nammet Beer - an older and stronger beer than those supplied at other times of the day

Nunchun - a lunch, or small meal taken between breakfast and dinner

Nuts - another name for Isle of Wight doughnuts

Oben Peel - a flat wooden shovel with a long handle used to put in or take out loaves from an oven

Oben Rubber - a pole with a cloth attached to clear wood-fired ovens of embers, before putting in the bread

Peak Hound - rock salmon / dogfish, also known as 'suss'

Pill - a jug or pitcher

Platter - a wooden plate, dish or trencher

Plump - to churn butter

Plumper - a butter churn

Prankle - a prawn

Puncheon - a small keg, containing from three pints to a gallon, used to carry beer into the fields at harvest time

Rammel Cheese - the best kind of cheese, made from whole milk

Ramsons / Ramsden - wild garlic, also known as 'gipsy onion'

Rarridge - radish

Rather Ripe - an early fruiting type of apple (from the Middle English word *rathe* meaning early)

Saaige - sage

Samper - samphire

Sand Sprat - the sand eel or sand lance (a small fish from the *Ammodytes* family)

Sassages - sausages

Scran Bag - a bag used by labourers to carry their food

Scrump - something baked hard, short in eating, like biscuits

Sharlott - shallot

Shrove Cakes - cakes given out on Shrove Tuesday to the children who would go singing from house to house

Skiver - a skewer, traditionally made from the wood of the Spindle Tree (*euonymus europaeus*) which was known as 'skiver wood'

Sorbus berries - chequers, the sharp-tasting fruit of the wild service tree (*sorbus torminalis*)

Sorrow - sorrel

Staabit - a 'staybit', a snack between meals, generally a piece of bread and cheese before dinner

Sterrup glass - a small glass of alcohol, drunk upon the horse before parting

Stubberds - an early fruiting variety of crab apple

Suss - rock salmon / dogfish, also known as 'peak hound'

Swizzle - small beer, ale and beer mixed together

Tackle - food and drink, also used for harnesses and agricultural equipment

Taffety - something that is delicate or dainty to eat

Thumbit - a piece of meat eaten on a piece of bread, so called from the thumb being placed on top of it

Turmet - turnip

Turmet Greens - turnip tops

Vlitters - small pancakes, fritters, also known as 'bletters'

Warlock - the black mustard plant (*sinapis nigra*)

Warnut - walnut

Whiting Cole - the pollock

Wight Spice - a local drink first advertised from 1888, made with 'nine of the choicest fragrant spices and wholesome Island fruits'. It could be drunk as it was or mixed with hot water, cold water, ale or stout.

Wild Celery - used both for wild celery (*apium graveolens*) but also for alexanders (*smyrnium olusatrum*)

Wild Spinage - sea beet (*beta maritima*)

Winter Kiksies / Winter Kecksies - sloes, the fruit of the blackthorn (*prunus spinosa*)

Wood Quest / Wood Quester - the wood pigeon

Wuts - oats

Zeed Cake - a seed cake, made in the wheat-sowing season

Zippet / Sippet - a small type of fried bread or French toast. One recipe gives directions to cut circles of bread using a tumbler and soak them in a mixture of milk and beaten egg for a few minutes. After that, fry them in butter and serve with jam.

Edible Wild Plants Native to the Island

This list uses the works of William Arnold Bromfield, Frederick Townsend and Charlotte O'Brien to detail some of the edible plants that were considered native to the Isle of Wight or had been naturalised by the 19th century. There is no certainty that Islanders definitely made use of all these plants however it is possible that they did.

Some of these species are now rare so always forage sustainably. Before eating any wild plants check you've identified them correctly and are aware of any effects they may have on your health.

Alexanders, *smyrnium olusatrum* (flowers, leaves, root, stem)
Asparagus, *asparagus officinalis* (stem)
Basil Thyme, *acinos arvensis* (leaves)
Bilberry, *vaccinium myrtillus* (fruit)
Blackberry, *rubus fruticosus* (fruit)
Blackcurrant, *ribes nigrum* (fruit, leaves)
Blackthorn, *prunus spinosa* (flowers, fruit)
Black Mustard, *brassica nigra* (leaves, seeds)

Borage, *borago officinalis* (flowers, leaves)

Burdock, *arctium lappa* (leaves)

Calamint, *calamintha nepeta* (leaves)

Chicory, *cichorium intybus* (flowers, leaves, root)

Common Mallow, *malva sylvestris* (seeds)

Common Parsley, *petroselinum crispum* (leaves)

Common Pear, *pyrus communis* (fruit)

Cowslip, *primula veris* (flowers)

Corn Parsley, *petroselinum segetum* (leaves)

Crab Apple, *malus sylvestris* (fruit)

Damson / Bullace, *prunus insititia* (fruit)

Dandelion, *taraxacum officinale* (flowers, leaves, root)

Dog Rose, *rosa canina* (petals, fruit)

Dog Violet, *viola canina* (petals)

Elder, *sambucus nigra* (flower, fruit)

Fennel, *foeniculum vulgare* (leaves, root, seeds, stem)

Field Maple, *acer campestre* (sap)

Field Poppy, *papaver rhoeas* (seeds)

Gillyflower, *matthiola incana* (flowers)

Goat's Beard, *tragopogon pratensis* (root, stem)

Golden Samphire, *inula crithmoides* (leaves)

Gooseberry, *ribes uva-crispa* (fruit)

Gorse, *ulex europaeus* (flowers)

Hawthorn, *crataegus monogyna* (flowers, fruit)

Hazel, *corylus avellana* (nuts)

Hedge Mustard, *sisymbrium officinale* (seeds)

Herb Bennet, *geum urbanum* (leaves, root)

Horehound, *marrubium vulgare* (leaves)

Horsemint, *mentha sylvestris* (leaves)

Horseradish, *armoracia rusticana* (root)

Lamb's Lettuce, *valerianella locusta* (leaves)

Land Cress, *barbarea verna* (leaves)

Marsh Mallow, *althaea officinalis* (leaves, root)

Meadowsweet, *filipendula ulmaria* (flowers, leaves)

Pignut, *conopodium majus* (root)

Plum, *prunus domestica* (fruit, flowers)

Primrose, *primula vulgaris* (flowers)

Raspberry, *rubus idaeus* (fruit)

Red Currant, *ribes rubrum* (fruit)

Rock Samphire, *crithmum maritimum* (leaves)

Roman Chamomile, *chamaemelum nobile* (flowers)

Round-Leaved Mint, *mentha rotundifolia* (leaves)

Salad Burnet, *sanguisorba minor* (leaves)

Sea Beet, *beta vulgaris maritima* (leaves)

Sea Kale, *crambe maritima* (leaves)

Sea Purslane, *halimione portulacoides* (leaves)

Sea Radish, *raphanus maritima* (leaves, root)

Sea Rocket, *cakile maritima* (flowers, leaves)

Sorrel, *rumex acetosa* (flowers, leaves)

Sour Cherry, *prunus cerasus* (fruit)

Small-Leaved Lime, *tilia cordata* (leaves, flowers)

Stinging Nettle, *urtica dioica* (leaves)

Sweet Chestnut, *castanea sativa* (nuts)

Sweet Violet, *viola odorata* (petals)

Sweet Woodruff, *galium odoratum* (leaves, flowers)

Sycamore, *acer psuedoplatanus* (sap)

Tansy, *tanacetum vulgare* (leaves, flowers)

Thyme, *thymus vulgaris* (flowers, leaves)

Wall Lettuce, *lactuca muralis* (leaves)

Watercress, *nasturtium officinale* (leaves)

Water Pepper, *polygonum hydropiper* (leaves)

White Birch, *betula alba* (sap)

White Mustard, *sinapis alba* (leaves, seeds)

Wild Angelica, *angelica sylvestris* (leaves, stem, root)

Wild Basil, *clinopodium vulgare* (leaves)

Wild Cabbage, *brassica oleracea* (leaves)

Wild Carrot, *daucus carota* (flowers, root)

Wild Cherry, *prunus avium* (fruit)

Wild Celery, *apium graveolens* (leaves, seeds)

Wild Garlic, *allium ursinum* (flowers, leaves, root)

Wild Marjoram, *origanum vulgare* (leaves)

Wild Parsnip, *pastinaca sativa* (root)

Wild Radish, *raphanus raphanistrum* (leaves, seeds)

Wild Sage, *salvia verbenaca* (flowers, leaves)

Wild Service Tree, *sorbus torminalis* (fruit)

Wild Strawberry, *fragaria vesca* (fruit)

Willowherb, *epilobium angustifolium* (leaves)

Wood Sorrel, *oxalis acetosella* (leaves, flowers)

Fried Pork

One of the most popular meals for 19th century Islanders was fried pork with cabbage and bacon. Sometimes other leaf vegetables were used too such as sea beet (pictured) or turnip tops.

Rosemary Cakes

On the Island, like in many other places, rosemary was associated with remembrance and special rosemary cakes, sometimes flavoured with spice, were traditionally eaten after a funeral.

Vlitters

Vlitters were a small type of pancake, similar to the Welsh and Scottish versions, that could be served with fruits like merries (wild cherries) and the Island's famously rich cream.

Isle of Wight Cracknels

Isle of Wight Cracknel Biscuits were possibly the Isle of Wight's most famous export, spreading across the globe during the Victorian era and even being produced in Tasmania and Calcutta.

Isle of Wight Junket

Two 19th century authors praised the Isle of Wight for its junket - a milky dessert, similar to a panna cotta. The name comes from the French word jonquette and they're sometimes flavoured with brandy, rose water or orange blossom.

Doughnuts

Isle of Wight Doughnuts have a plum-filled centre with a sweet and spicy casing. Also known as 'nuts', they're unrelated to the American version and some claim they can be traced as far back as the 17th century.

Apple Stucklens

Apple Stucklens were a small semi-circular pastry filled with sliced apples and sugar, often eaten at harvest time. They may have used crab apples or even the Island's own variety of apple: the Isle of Wight Pippin.

Sloe Ice

In the 1840s ices were supplied for Cowes Regatta by Gunter's of Berkeley Square, London. By the 1850s Isle of Wight confectioners were making them too and could have even used local fruits, like this sloe flavoured ice.

Recipes

Rosemary Cakes

Rosemary was a herb especially associated with remembrance on the Isle of Wight and at least a couple of references are made to a special rosemary flavoured 'cake' baked for funerals, sometimes containing spice too. The day after the ceremony half a dozen of these cakes would be sent to the clergyman wrapped in a white cloth, which would suggest they were fairly small, but apart from that little is known as no recipe seems to exist.

The following recipe uses the information available to best recreate what these rosemary cakes may have looked like. If each cut-out of the rolled dough is left flat it creates a scone shape but if it's shaped into a ball, the cake is much rounder.

Makes about 16

500g strong white bread flour
80g unsalted butter, cubed
4 sprigs of rosemary, finely chopped with stalks removed
150g grated cheese
250ml milk
2 medium eggs
5 tsp baking powder
1 tsp sea salt

1. Sift 450g of the flour into a mixing bowl, add the cubed butter and rub it in with your fingers until it becomes the consistency of breadcrumbs. Add the rosemary, cheese, eggs, salt and baking powder and mix with a wooden spoon.

2. Add 125ml of the milk and gently turn the mixture to combine. Add as much of the remaining milk as needed, a little at a time, continuing to work by hand until it forms a soft sticky dough.

3. Use half of the remaining flour to dust the work surface and turn the dough out onto it. Flatten the dough and sprinkle the other 25g of flour on top of it. Fold the dough in half, then turn it 90 degrees and repeat until all the flour is mixed in and the dough becomes smooth.

4. Dust the work surface again and gently roll the dough out until it's around 2.5cm thick. Use a small pastry cutter or the rim of a small glass to stamp out rounds and place them on a baking tray.

5. Optional: For a rounder rosemary cake, make the stamped out circle into a ball by stretching it with your thumbs, bringing the edges together in one place and pinching them to seal. Then place the ball back onto the baking tray with the join underneath.

6. Brush the tops with milk or beaten eggs and sprinkle with a little extra cheese.

7. Bake at 220°C for about 15 minutes until risen and golden. Tap the base of each cake to listen for a hollow sound to know they're done. Cool on a wire rack.

Apple Stucklen

Apple Stucklens were a small pastry filled with apples and baked without a dish. The most common form seems to have been similar to an apple turnover but semicircular in shape, with sliced apples and sugar folded inside the pastry. However, the term also seems to have been used for apple pies or tarts that were baked in the same way. Apple stucklens are mentioned in a few novels by local author Maxwell Gray (1846 - 1923), who describes how they were taken into the fields by gleaners at harvest time.

It's likely that Isle of Wight Pippins or wild apples were used, with a number of varieties available to Islanders including stubberds, rather ripe and crumplens. Similar apple-based desserts known as stucklings could also historically be found in Hampshire, Surrey and Sussex.

Makes 6

375g puff pastry or shortcrust pastry
3 medium apples, sliced, peeled and cored
75g of light brown sugar or golden caster sugar
25g of unsalted butter
The zest of a lemon
Cinnamon, to taste (optional)
Whole milk for glazing

1. Melt the butter in a saucepan before adding the sliced apple, lemon zest and 1 tablespoon of water. Cook for around 5 minutes, or until the apple has softened.

2. Roll the puff pastry out on a lightly floured surface until it's half a centimetre in thickness. Using the rim of a glass or a circular pastry cutter, cut out as many circles as you can from the puff pastry.

3. Place just under half a tablespoon of the apple mixture on one side of each pastry circle, leaving a border around the edge. Sprinkle the apple with ½ tsp of golden caster sugar or light brown sugar and a pinch of cinnamon.

4. Brush the border with milk then bring the empty side of the pastry over the filled side and press the edges together. Crimp the edge for a more decorative finish. Cut two small slits on the top of the stucklen for steam to escape and transfer them to a baking sheet or tin, lined with baking paper.

5. Brush each stucklen with whole milk to glaze and sprinkle over any remaining sugar.

6. Bake at 180°C until puffed up and golden. Leave to cool on a wire rack before serving.

Seed Cake

Locally pronounced 'zeed cake', this special type of cake was traditionally made on the Island during the wheat-sowing season. This recipe uses caraway seeds but other types of seeds may have been used as well.

200g plain flour
200g unsalted butter, cubed and softened
200g caster sugar
4 large eggs
2 tbsp brandy
1 tbsp caraway seeds
1 tbsp nutmeg
½ tsp baking powder
Zest of a lemon

1. Beat the butter and sugar together in a bowl using an electric whisk until pale and fluffy. Then beat in the eggs one by one.

2. Sift the flour and baking powder into a separate bowl and add in the lemon zest, nutmeg and caraway seeds.

3. Gradually fold the dry mixture into the wet mixture, using a spatula, until evenly combined.

4. Next, fold in the brandy. The mixture should now be soft enough to drop off the spoon when shaken. If it's too dry, add a small amount of milk to get the right consistency.

5. Transfer the mixture to a greased cake tin (one around 20cm wide will do) and bake at 180°C for between 45 and 50 minutes. Check it's done by pressing a skewer into the middle of the cake, if it comes out clean, the cake is ready.

6. Leave to cool in the tin for 15 minutes before removing the cake and placing it on a wire rack to cool further.

Isle of Wight Cracknels

Based on a recipe first published in 1808. Isle of Wight Cracknel biscuits are very difficult to make correctly. The Georgian recipes give no exact quantities for the sugar or the nutmeg, they don't indicate what exactly 'cracknel shapes' might be and the cooking instructions are simply given as bake 'in an oven sufficiently brisk to make them crisp, but not by any means high coloured'.

The most difficult part is boiling the raw biscuits and then thoroughly drying them. It's easy for them to lose their shape at this stage and if they're not dry enough when they're baked they won't turn out as intended. However, although less in keeping with tradition, the boiling stage can be missed out, which will result in a crumblier biscuit, more similar in texture to a shortbread. If you're feeling brave enough to try the original recipe though, it might be worth baking for a shorter time at a higher temperature.

Makes about 10

200g plain flour, sifted
140g unsalted butter, cubed
1 egg yolk, beaten
1 egg white, beaten
1 dessert spoon of caster sugar
1 ½ tsp rose water or orange-flower water
½ tsp ground nutmeg

1. Sift the flour into a mixing bowl. Separately beat one egg yolk and combine it with the nutmeg, sugar and either orange-flower water or rose water, before adding it to the flour and mixing together.

2. Next, gradually mix in the softened butter and then start rolling the dough until it becomes soft and smooth.

3. Once it's reached the right consistency, roll the dough to just under 1cm in thickness and using a small cutter, stamp out the biscuits.

4. (Optional) Bring a saucepan of water to the boil and once bubbling put the raw biscuits into the pan. Once they swim to the surface take them out and plunge them into cold water to harden. After this, dry them slowly and thoroughly.

5. Whether you chose to boil them or not, brush the biscuits with the beaten egg white and place on a greased tin or baking sheet.

6. Cook at 150°C for around 20 minutes on a low shelf. They should remain fairly pale and not turn too golden. Once cooked, leave to cool on a wire rack.

Isle of Wight Doughnuts

Based on a recipe of 1845. Also known as 'nuts', they were traditionally boiled in melted lard and drained on clean straw. The original version used allspice, cinnamon, cloves and mace in the dough and small wild plums as the filling - which gave rise to them also being known as 'birds' nests'. Later recipes use just nutmeg in the dough and currants to fill them. These doughnuts have a delicious dough with the taste and texture of a spicy brown bread which goes really well with the rich, plummy filling.

Makes 10

300g strong white bread flour
150 - 175ml whole milk
50g unsalted butter, cubed
50g fine brown sugar or light muscovado, sieved
7g sachet of instant yeast
2 tsp. allspice
¼ tsp. cinnamon
a pinch of ground cloves
a pinch of ground mace
½ tsp salt
Vegetable oil for deep frying

Filling:
Either - pitted wild plums / chopped supermarket plums with the stone removed / plum jam piped into the doughnut OR a mixture of 2 tbsp currants 1 tbsp mixed candied peel and ¼ tsp ground cinnamon.

1. Sift the flour and spices into a bowl, adding the salt and sugar on one side of the mixture and the yeast on the other. Add the softened butter and 120ml of the milk then combine by hand. Gradually add as much of the remaining milk as you need until the dough is soft and slightly tacky.

2. Knead the dough on a flour dusted surface until smooth and no longer sticky. Oil the bowl, return the dough to it and cover, leaving it somewhere warm to rise until it has doubled in size.

3. Line two metal baking trays with baking parchment. Place the dough back on a floured work surface and fold inwards until the air is knocked out and the dough is smooth. Divide into ten pieces and roll into balls.

4. Make a hole in each ball of dough with the thumb and push a little of the filling inside. Stretch the dough over the hole to close it, pinching and twisting the join to seal it. Once filled, place the balls on the baking trays and cover for 45 minutes to double in size. They should ultimately be about the size of a cricket ball.

5. Deep fry the balls, a few at a time for around seven minutes, until cooked through and a fine brown in colour. Turn them over half way through to ensure even colouring

6. Remove the doughnuts from the pan with a slotted spoon, drain on kitchen paper and leave to cool.

Junket

An ancient milk-based dessert, a bit like panna cotta, said to take its name from the French word 'jonquette'. It has existed in Britain since at least the medieval period and still has strong associations with the West Country. The Isle of Wight was supposedly renowned for its junkets, which were typically covered in an inch-thick layer of clotted cream. Historically they were served in a large ceramic bowl known as a 'basin' and often eaten with fruit.

Serves 4 - 5

500 ml of whole milk (preferably from Jersey or Guernsey cattle)
Flavouring such as ½ tbsp brandy or ½ tsp. orange flower or rosewater (optional)
1 tbsp. caster sugar (optional)
1 tsp. liquid vegetarian rennet
Nutmeg or cinnamon to dust
Clotted cream

1. Heat the milk, a generous pinch of nutmeg and any other flavouring in a saucepan to 37°C (body temperature).

2. Add the rennet and stir it quickly throughout the mixture before pouring it into a china bowl or individual portion-sized glasses.

3. Allow to set for around 15 minutes at room temperature then chill in the fridge for an hour before serving. Dust with nutmeg or cinnamon and serve with clotted cream and fruit.

Vlitter Pancakes

Vlitters, also known as bletters or flitters, were a type of small pancake. They were not as thin or wide as a crêpe and probably more closely resembled Scotch pancakes or the Welsh crempog pancakes. On Shrove Tuesday, if households on the Island ran out of Shrove Cakes to give to the singers going door to door, then these pancakes or doughnuts were often given instead. Some of these Shrove Tuesday traditions have strong similarities with those of Wales which may suggest a Celtic origin.

This name wasn't totally unique to the Isle of Wight and records of small 'flitter' pancakes also exist in Devon. As with many of the Island's historic foods, it seems no recipe has survived, so the following is a recreation of what they might have looked like.

Makes 10

225g self-raising flour, sifted
250ml whole milk
25g caster sugar
40g butter, melted
1 medium egg
2 tsp vegetable oil

1. Sift the flour and sugar into a mixing bowl. Make a well in the middle and add the melted butter, egg and 125ml of the whole milk. Mix together, slowly adding the rest of the milk until it creates a smooth, thick batter.

2. Lightly oil a frying pan and heat. Drop two or three tablespoons of mixture into the pan at a time to make a pancake roughly 8cm wide. Cook as many as you can fit in your pan, for between a minute and a minute and a half, or until bubbles appear on the surface.

3. Flip the pancakes and cook for a further minute until golden, crisp and puffy.

4. Cool on a wire rack and cover with a clean tea towel while you make the rest.

5. Serve with whipped cream, fruit, honey or treacle. For a savoury version add bacon and cheese.

Isle of Wight Food Today

Today the Island's food culture is very different, being renowned instead - both locally and nationally - for the quality of its homegrown ingredients such as speciality tomatoes and a diverse range of different garlics. Interestingly, both of these particular crops (knowingly or not) still contain echoes of the past.

For about thirty years, tomatoes have been grown commercially in the Arreton Valley but their story on the Isle of Wight does stretch back a bit further in time. In the late 19th century, tomatoes were starting to make an appearance in the county, perhaps encouraged by the new wave of European chefs and hoteliers, such as Hubert Cloots, a native of Belgium, who grew them in his unheated greenhouses at The Royal Hotel as far back as 1900.

Similarly, the now famous Isle of Wight Garlic echoes the local Romani gypsy tradition of eating wild garlic as well as adding another French strand to Island food. In a way, it continues the story of oysters from Brittany, apples from Normandy and smuggled French spirits which were introduced to create some of the most distinctive Isle of Wight products of the 18th and 19th centuries.

The first bulbs of French garlic that started the ball rolling for this family business made their way to the Island at the height of the Second World War and the story of their journey is truly incredible.

In 1942, around 300 French sailors were stationed at Cowes with their squadron of torpedo boats and they often used to drink at The Painters Arms in Cross Street, where many of them supposedly complained to the landlord, Bill Spidy, about how much they missed French garlic. The landlord spoke to his friends in the Air Force and contact was made with RAF Tangmere in Sussex to see if anything could be done. Luckily they took the request seriously, seeing how it could boost morale amongst the Free French, so they put a plan into operation.

On the 27th October, RAF pilots, supposedly working with British double agent Mary Lindell, carried out a night mission to Central France and managed to bring back a sack of Auvergne garlic from the fields of Clermont-Ferrand. Back on the Island, the landlord planted the garlic and gave some to his neighbour, Norah Boswell of Mersley Farm, who grew it in her kitchen garden for many years and whose descendants now run The Garlic Farm, so well known on the Island today.

These new features of modern Isle of Wight food are certainly something to be proud of however this doesn't mean historic Island food has no place in today's local culinary culture - there's definitely room to accommodate both. What's more, reviving the Island's culinary heritage can enhance and expand on the foodie traits that already attract so much interest from the rest of the country.

In the same way that no trip to Cornwall is complete without a Cornish pasty, the Isle of Wight's spicy plum-filled doughnuts could be revived and become a similarly synonymous food product. Or in the same way that visitors to the Lake District might come home with some Grasmere Gingerbread as a souvenir, Isle of Wight Cracknels could fulfil a similar role here.

There are also lessons to be learnt about the enormous value Islanders put on the wild plants and the multitude of uses they found for them. As the Island strives to become more environmentally friendly in future, preservation of these biologically and culturally important plants should be a serious consideration.

Of course, no work like this can be called complete and there is still a wealth of Isle of Wight food history to be properly unearthed and examined. For example, what exactly were the *Hallan Cakes* made by Islanders on the 1st of November and what ingredients made up Payne's Royal Osborne Sauce, a 'piquant' and 'exquisite condiment' made by a Cowes chemist, sold at Fortnum & Mason and displayed at the Great Exhibition of 1851.

Similarly, there are other stories which don't neatly fit into traditional Isle of Wight food but deserve some recognition too such as the founding of Horniman's Tea in Newport in 1826.

The company was established on the Island by John Horniman, a Quaker from Reading, who set up the first company in Britain to sell pure, pre-packaged and branded tea. At the time, tea was sold loose at grocers and to improve profit margins the expensive tea leaves were often mixed with dust, hawthorn leaves or even hedge clippings to make it go further and dye was used to disguise poor quality ingredients. Horniman's Pure Tea was the only brand found to contain no trace of dye by *The Lancet* and the business soon developed a reputation for quality, moving to London and by 1891 becoming the biggest-selling tea brand in Britain.

Time will tell how many other stories of historic Isle of Wight food there are to discover but what's clear is that there are more than enough interesting features to make Island food distinctive and worthy of recognition. What's more, if the modern innovations that characterise Isle of Wight food now are enhanced by revived historic and cultural food traditions, the Island's regional cuisine could become something truly extraordinary.

Bibliography

Acton, Eliza. Modern Cookery, In All Its Branches (1845)

Adams, William Henry Davenport. Nelson's Handbook to the Isle of Wight (1873)

Adams, William Henry Davenport. The History, Topography and Antiquities of the Isle of Wight (1856)

Albin, John (Pub.). A New, Correct, and Much-Improved History of the Isle of Wight (1795)

Albin, John (Pub.). A Companion to the Isle of Wight (1799)

Albin, John (Pub.). Sketches of Description, Taken On Sailing from Newport in the Isle of Wight to Lymington: With a Return by Southampton to Cowes (1792)

Allen, Lake. The History of Portsmouth (1817)

Anon. Bradshaw's Shilling Handbook (1858)

Anon. Industrial Great Britain; A Commercial Review of Leading Firms, Selected from Important Towns of England (1854)

Anon. Murray's Modern Cookery Book. Modern Domestic Cookery (1851)

Anon. "Oyster Fisheries of the Isle of Wight", The Board of Trade Journal, Vol. 1 (1887)

Anon. The Royal Umbrella: A Ballad of the Isle of Wight (1844)

Atkins, Henry. The Isle of Wight: a Poem, with Other Pieces in Verse (1837)

Beeton, Isabella (Mrs. Beeton). The Book of Household Management (1861)

Bickerdyke, John. Sea Fishing (1895)

Blessington, Marguerite. A Tour in the Isle of Wight in the Autumn of 1820 (1822)

Bromfield, William Arnold. Flora Vectensis; Being a Systematic Description of the Phaenogamous or Flowering Plants and Ferns Indigenous to the Isle of Wight (1856)

Chambers, Vincent (Ed.) Old Men Remember; Life on Victoria's Smaller Island (1988)

Chrystal, Paul. Tea: A Very British Beverage (2014)

Coles, William. Adam in Eden, or Nature's Paradise: The History of Plants, Fruits, Herbs and Flowers (1657)

Cooke, William. A New Picture of the Isle of Wight (1808)

Cooper, James Fenimore. Recollections of Europe, Volume 1 (1837)

Demorest, William Jennings. Demorest's Monthly Magazine, Volume 21 (1885)

Ditchfield, P. H. Picturesque English Cottages and their Doorway Gardens (1905)

Ellison, Edith Nicholl. A Child's Recollections of Tennyson (1906)

Fielding, Henry. The Journal of a Voyage to Lisbon (1755)

Fisher, Judith L. "Tea and Food Adulteration, 1834 - 75" Britain, Representation and Nineteenth-Century History. Ed. Dino Franco Felluga (2012)

Gilpin, William. Observations on the Western Parts of England, Relative Chiefly to Picturesque Beauty (1798)

Garle, Hubert. A Driving Tour of the Isle of Wight (1905)

Gray, Annie. The Greedy Queen: Eating with Victoria (2017)

Halliwell-Philipps, James Orchard. A Dictionary of Archaic and Provincial Words, Obsolete Phrases, and Ancient Customs (1847)

Halliwell-Phillips, James Orchard. Popular Rhymes and Nursery Tales (1849)

Hargrove, Ethel C. Wanderings in the Isle of Wight (1913)

Hassell, John. Tour of the Isle of Wight, Volume 2 (1790)

Hillier, George. The Topography of the Isle of Wight (1854)

Hogg, Robert. British Pomology: or, The History, Description, Classification, and Synonyms, of the Fruits and Fruit Trees of Great Britain (1851)

Horsey, Samuel (Pub.). The Isle of Wight Visitor's Book (1839)

Hunwick, Heather Delancey. Doughnut: A Global History (2015)

Isle of Wight County Federation of Women's Institutes. Isle of Wight Cookery Book (1934)

Jenkinson, Henry Irwin. Jenkinson's Practical Guide to the Isle of Wight (1883)

Jones, Jack & Johanna Jones. The Isle of Wight. An Illustrated History (1987)

Lambert, William. The Vectis Directory, or General Isle of Wight Guide (1839)

Lewis, Samuel. A Topographical Dictionary of England (1831)

Long, William Henry. A Dictionary of the Isle of Wight Dialect, and of Provincialisms Used in the Island (1886)

Longman, Charles James (Ed.) Longman's Magazine, Volume 35 (1900)

Lovell, M.S. The Edible Mollusks of Great Britain (1867)

Luxford, George & Edward Newman (Eds.). The Phytologist: a Popular Botanical Miscellany, Volume 3 (1842)

Luxford, George & Edward Newman (Eds.). The Phytologist: a Popular Botanical Miscellany, Volume 3, Part 2 (1849)

Macallan, Emma. Stories Descriptive of the Isle of Wight (1859)

MacDonald, Duncan. The New London Family Cook: Or, Town and Country Housekeeper's Guide (1808)

Martin, George Anne. The Undercliff. Its Climate, History and Natural Productions (1849)

Maund, Henry. Sandown, Isle of Wight, as a Residence and as a Health Resort (1867)

Mogridge, George (pseudonym Old Humphrey). Owen Gladdon's Wanderings in the Isle of Wight (1850)

Morey, Frank. A Guide to the Natural History of the Isle of Wight (1909)

O'Brien, Charlotte. Wild Flowers of the Undercliff, Isle of Wight (1881)

Panayi, Panikos. Migrant City: A New History of London (2020)

Parker-Bowles, Tom. Full English: A Journey Through the British and Their Food (2009)

Radcliffe, M. A Modern System of Domestic Cookery: or, The Housekeeper's Guide &c. (1839)

Raine, Rosa. The Queen's Isle, Chapters on the Isle of Wight (1861)

Richards, John Morgan. Almost Fairyland: Personal Notes Concerning the Isle of Wight (1914)

Smith, Major Henry & Charles Roach Smith. Original Glossaries, Series C, XXIII - Isle of Wight Words (1881)

Tomkins, Charles. A Tour to the Isle of Wight, Volumes 1 & 2 (1796)

Townsend, Frederick. Flora of Hampshire, including the Isle of Wight (1883)

Tuttiett, Mary Gleed (pseudonym Maxwell Gray). Ribstone Pippins (1898)

Tuttiett, Mary Gleed (pseudonym Maxwell Gray). Unconfessed (1911)

Vancouver, Charles. General View of the Agriculture of Hampshire, including the Isle of Wight (1810)

Various. Notes and Queries: A Medium of Intercommunication for Literary Men, Artists, Antiquaries, Genealogists etc. Second Series, Volume 8 (1859)

Various. On Oyster Culture in Relation to Disease (1896)

Various. Proceedings of the Isle of Wight History and Archaeological Society, Vol 3. (1938)

Various. The Mirror of Literature, Amusement, and Instruction, Volume 18 (1831)

Various. Vegetarian Messenger, Volumes 2 - 10 (1851)

Vaughan, John. The Wild Flowers of Selborne and Other Papers (1906)

Vectis, Philo (pseudonym) The Isle of Wight Tourist, and Companion at Cowes (1830)

Venables, Edmund. The Isle of Wight, a Guide (1860)

W. Kelly & Co. Post Office London Directory for 1902 (1902)

Warner, Richard. The History of the Isle of Wight, Military, Ecclesiastical, Civil & Natural (1795)

Wilcocks, J. The Sea-Fisherman or Fishing Pilotage (1865)

Wright, Joseph (Ed.) The English Dialect Dictionary, Volume 1 (1898)

Wright, Joseph (Ed.) The English Dialect Dictionary, Volume 2 (1900)

Wright, Joseph (Ed.) The English Dialect Dictionary, Volume 4 (1905)

Wright, Joseph (Ed.) The English Dialect Dictionary, Volume 5 (1905)

Youatt, William. Cattle: Their Breeds, Management, and Diseases (1834)

Ysewijn, Regula. Oats in the North, Wheat from the South (2020)

Belfast Commercial Chronicle, 13 February 1839
Daily Mail, 31 July 2018
Devizes and Wiltshire Gazette, 01 February 1855
Essex Standard, 06 May 1842
Friend of India Statesman, 12 July 1855
Friend of India Statesman, 26 February 1863
Hampshire Independent, 10 January 1880
Hampshire Telegraph, Multiple Issues
Hastings and St. Leonards Observer, 27 July 1878
Home News for India, China and the Colonies, 08 July 1850
Isle of Wight County Press, Multiple Issues
Isle of Wight Observer, Multiple Issues
Isle of Wight Times, Multiple Issues
John O'Groat Journal, 10 March 1843
Liverpool Daily Post, 20 September 1870
Liverpool Mail, 06 December 1851
Norfolk News, 19 December 1846
Oxford Journal, 12 September 1840
Saunders's News-Letter, 13 October 1846
The Courier, Hobart Town [Tasmania], 27 May 1845
The Scotsman, 21 December 1836
Wolverhampton Chronicle and Staffordshire Advertiser, 31
    January 1844

About the Author

James Rayner was born and brought up on the Isle of Wight. His background is in language and literature which he studied with the University of Iceland and the University of Malmö in Sweden. His first book, *The Isle of Wight's Missing Chapter* was published in 2019 and focused on the Island's forgotten Asian, African and Caribbean history.